Commanders In Crisis: The Psychological Battles of American Presidents Throughout History

Joseph Collins

Published by Night Writer Publishing, 2024.

While every precaution has been taken in the preparation of this book, the publisher assumes no responsibility for errors or omissions, or for damages resulting from the use of the information contained herein.

COMMANDERS IN CRISIS: THE PSYCHOLOGICAL BATTLES OF AMERICAN PRESIDENTS THROUGHOUT HISTORY

First edition. September 15, 2024.

ISBN: 979-8227011794

Written by Joseph Collins.

Table of Contents

Preface

The late Dr. James Barber of Duke University knew a few things about American presidents. Early in his career, he served in the U.S. Army as a Counterintelligence Agent. In that role, he trained extensively in Personality Theory and Advanced Interrogation Techniques. His studies and experiences in the field provided him with a deep understanding of various personality types; taught him profiling techniques in order to understand what drives and motivates people; and informed him on the ways in which cultural influences can have an impact on personalities. After his tenure in the military, Barber obtained masters and doctorate degrees in Political Science and settled into a career applying personality theory to the movers and shakers of American politics.

In 1972 he published, *The Presidential Character: Predicting Performance in the White House*, a book in which he took the position that presidential personalities can be broken down into four basic personality type combinations:
Active Positive
Passive Negative

Active-Positive: having a readiness to act on behalf of the nation, high optimism, and an overall appreciation for the integrity of the office of the presidency.

Active-Negative: lacking a sense of commitment to the work of the presidency, aggressive, highly rigid, and one who uses power for his or her own advancement and selfish goals.

Passive-Positive: possessing a low self-esteem compensated by an ingratiating personality, superficially optimistic, and a desire to please.

Passive-Negative: having a strong sense of duty, desire to avoid power, low self-esteem compensated by service towards others, and an overall aversion to intense political negotiation.

IN HIS BOOK, BARBER accurately predicted candidate Richard Nixon would win the presidency. Based on his assessment of Nixon's personality profile, he predicted Nixon would abuse power and display traits of neuroticism and insecurity. The young professor boldly stated in a *Time* magazine interview regarding the upcoming election,

> "the choice was between an Active-Positive, George McGovern, and a psychologically defective Active-Negative, Richard Nixon."

Nixon would go on to win a second term for president. However, Barber's prediction emerged in full bloom when Nixon fell from grace by taping government offices and committing his aides to the Watergate break-in of the Democratic Party headquarters. He quickly became one of the most credible authorities in the country on the American presidency.

In my preparation of this book, I have relied on the assessment tools of Professor Barber, my own training and experience as a mental health counselor, as well as the research and writings of a host of other psychologists, historians and psychobiographers. The bibliography I have relied on is extensive and I am grateful for the hard work of all those who researched and published before me.

The scope and purpose of *Commanders In Crisis* is three-fold. I want to distill important lessons about mental health and stimulate a positive conversation about the importance of emotional well-being and informed self-care for everyone. I do this in part through the major findings of psychiatrists, psychologists, psychobiographers, presidential scholars and historians regarding the diagnoses and health narratives of American presidents and their families. In the process of sharing my findings, I reject any and all attempts to draw broad conclusions relating to political parties (historical or contemporary), cultural identities, or other personal differences.

As I share this manuscript, I remain indebted to my own former colleagues in the Intelligence community and health care fields. Many of you continue to work tirelessly as analysts, mental health professionals, chemical dependency counselors, peer counselors; chaplains in the hospice and hospital arenas; HIV Planning Council members and others who serve people living with HIV/AIDS; physicians, nurses, and patient aides. You have taught me invaluable lessons over the years. I pray your strength, empathy and compassion will never fail as you seek to protect this nation and help those in your care.

Introduction

THIS BOOK, *Commanders In Crisis* is a brief historical survey of the most severe mental health diagnoses that have impacted American presidents from George Washington to Richard Nixon. It is organized in six major sections, each section designed to introduce and discuss a major mental health diagnosis. In these sections, White House executives that battled one or more serious mental health diagnoses are profiled in the context of the period in which they lived, served and the historic events that shaped their administrations.

In addition to their historical environment, each of these American presidents are also discussed according to the stages of mental health services delivery and reform periods in their lifetimes. This helps to shed light on the availability of mental health services to these presidents and other Americans during their lifetimes.

Historical Stages of Mental Health Services Delivery and Reform

THE PRE-1820 ERA OF Mental Health Services in America & Europe

The treatment of people with psychosis and serious mental health disorders prior to 1820 was nothing short of medieval and cruel. It involved superstitious and untrained hacks experimenting on people's bodies; forcing patients to ingest substances which were ineffective and possibly toxic; and involved warehousing patients away from family and society in jails, prisons and other unconscionable conditions. Many were also homeless, hungry and abused in America's streets and rural communities.

THE MORAL TREATMENT era (1820's to 1890)

As America broke free of European colonialism, the social and religious reform movements sweeping the nation began to emphasize moral discipline, humane care and the value of a therapeutic, structured environment. Freestanding asylums and almshouses were built to accomplish these goals. The cruelty and brutal experimentation of the previous era was no longer the rule but effective therapy remained an unfulfilled aspiration due to a lack of established scientific methods and properly trained professionals.

THE MENTAL HYGIENE movement (1890 to 1940)

During the mid to late 1800s, the research of Sigmund Freud, Carl Jung and Adolf Meyer were having a major impact on the Western medical community. A cadre of science-minded clinicians emerged and began to define mental hygiene "as the biological or pathological origins for mental illness; and linked psychiatry with neurology, biology, and physiology." Psychopathic hospitals and clinics were built around the United States and the medical community made modest gains in their attempt to merge moral treatment with mental health science.

THE COMMUNITY MENTAL Health Reform period (World War II to late 1970's)

This reform period produced the concept of community mental health centers as emotionally wounded men and women returned home from WWII. Politicians, physicians and the general public were not willing to tolerate the remote treatment of veterans in psychiatric facilities far away from their families. As a result, treatment improved and antipsychotic medications were also introduced for the first time to effectively treat those clients with serious psychosis.

———

THE COMMUNITY SUPPORT Reform era (late 1970's to the present)

The push to deliver mental health services in communities was extended to caring for clients in their own homes and using natural support systems. The reforms embraced the idea of providing safe housing for indigent clients, case management services, transportation, employment and education services in order to assist clients to live more productive lives. This model of care continues today and most recently includes the principles of person-centered, recovery-oriented, trauma-informed and culturally competent care in the delivery of all services.

———

IN ADDITION TO THIS book discussing the mental health diagnoses and social reform periods in which these American presidents lived, I have also explored the traumas, personal losses and grief experienced by these executives down through the ages. My research shows that the loss of multiple siblings and parents during a president's childhood had the potential to devastate their lives and emotional wellness for decades to come. The same is true for the deaths of presidents' children. In this text I not only show how these emotional forces have negatively impacted the psychological well-being of executives - they can also influence policy decisions and even destroy presidential administrations.

Chapter One: Bipolar Disorder

―――

"Bipolar robs you of that which is you. It can take from you the very core of your being and replace it with something that is completely opposite of who and what you truly are. Because my bipolar went untreated for so long, I spent many years looking in the mirror and seeing a person I did not recognize or understand."

- Alyssa Reyans, Author of *Letters from a Bipolar Mother*

―――

Introduction

IN THE COURSE OF AMERICAN history, the presidency has been a stage upon which the complexities of human nature are magnified. Among the myriad challenges faced by those who have held this esteemed office, the burden of mental health has been an enduring thread. Exploring their lives illuminates not only the personal struggles of these individuals but also the intersection of mental health and leadership at the highest echelons of power. In our examination of Bipolar Disorder in former U.S. presidents, we will summarize in layman terms the elements of the disease and profile the life of an executive who suffered from its impact. Lastly, we will identify other former executives who were impacted by Bipolar Disorder.

―――

Diagnostic Summary

IMAGINE YOUR EMOTIONS are like a roller coaster ride. Sometimes you feel really excited and happy, like you're flying high at the top of the coaster. Other times, you might feel really sad and low, like you're stuck at the bottom. Bipolar Disorder is a lot like riding that roller coaster, but your highs and lows are much bigger and can happen more often. When someone has Bipolar Disorder, they experience extreme mood swings. They might feel super energetic and on top of the world during a "high" period, called mania. But then, they might suddenly feel incredibly sad and hopeless during a "low" period, called depression. It's as if their emotions are on a wild ride that's hard to control.

A Presidential Profile: John Adams

A depiction of President John Adams in a meeting with his advisors (circa 1800)

THE PRESIDENT BECAME the target of a renowned journalist who garnered national attention for exposing the eccentricities of politicians and other luminaries of his day. The journalist once wrote,

> "As President, he has never opened his lips or lifted his pen without threatening and scolding; the grand object of his administration has been to exasperate the rage of contending parties ... and destroy[ing] every man who differs from his opinions."

This same politician once proposed legislation making it illegal for others to criticize him or his allies and justified it on "national security" grounds. He raged at his political opponents by calling them childish names, challenging the dignity of their parentage and fantasized out loud about jailing his enemies. While this may sound curiously familiar, this description is not about anyone in the recent news or even living in this century. The executive being profiled is none other than the second holder of the American presidency, John Adams.

Hailed as one of the brightest and hardest-working intellectuals to ever hold office, the first President Adams is also remembered for being incredibly thin-skinned, vengeful and a name-calling "madman." His life, words and historical record have also been evaluated many times from a psychological perspective. It is almost universally agreed that he suffered from Bipolar II Disorder, at times referred to as "manic-depressive disorder."

John Adams was a temperamental, angry and disagreeable politician to the extent that it negatively impacted his career on a regular basis. His contemporaries referred to him in surprisingly harsh terms:

> "sometimes absolutely mad!"

> -Thomas Jefferson

> "always an honest man, often a wise one, but sometimes and in some things, absolutely out of his senses."

> - Benjamin Franklin

His explosive behavior and intolerance of being criticized played a major role in his losing the opportunity to become America's first president. He lost that honor to George Washington and had to settle for becoming the first Vice President of the United States. While Adams once referred to Washington as a "muttonhead" and stated that he was,

"too illiterate, unlearned, [and] unread for his station and reputation,"

even that was not his greatest indiscretion at the time.

He proposed the Alien & Sedition Act as a Federalist congressman and actually succeeded in getting it passed into law. This was one of the biggest factors in him being dropped from the short list for First President of the United States. Several people were actually imprisoned by this law that made it a crime to speak critical statements about other politicians and leaders. Despite his success in ensuring people were jailed for statements against him and his party, John Adams could not restrain himself from calling Alexander Hamilton,

". . . a bastard brat of a Scotch ped[d]ler."

To his credit, Adams was a gifted and energetic writer. As a graduate of Harvard University and an attorney, he spent his early years in politics helping America break free of Britain's stranglehold and learning to stand on its own. He was the primary author of the Massachusetts Constitution which later became a blueprint for the U.S. Constitution. He collaborated with his friend Thomas Jefferson to hammer out the Declaration of Independence and penned several other books and essays on how a new nation called America should be governed. As a diplomat stationed in several European capitals, John Adams along with his son John Quincy Adams (who was later elected sixth US President), spent years advocating on behalf of the struggling new nation and earned his place in history as a Founding Father.

Nevertheless, Adams' professional legacy is not complete without understanding his lifelong struggle with Bipolar II Disorder. His condition of mood swings included bursts of energy which fueled his prolific writing, as well as angry outbursts that garnered the ire of fellow politicians and diplomats. His episodes of severe depression at times left him bedridden and nearly catatonic.

The Adams Family Legacy

BIPOLAR DISORDER HAS a high tendency to be passed down in families through the genetic line. In fact, modern psychiatrists have found that Bipolar Disorder is more likely to be passed down from parent-to-child than any other psychiatric condition. The early Adams family was no exception. Charles Francis Adams is the great-grandson of the second president and grandson of the sixth. He once wrote,

> "The history of my family is not a pleasant one to remember. It is one of the great triumphs of the world but of deep groans within, one of extraordinary brilliancy and deep corroding mortification."

The "corroding mortification" was what the elder Adams himself made reference to several times in his diary entries. He called it "anxiety and distress." John and Abigail Adams gave birth to their first son, John Quincy Adams who suffered from Major Depression most of his life. He apparently found ways to curb the more extreme excesses of his disease, became President of the United States and lived to be 80 years old. Their second child, Charles Adams followed in the footsteps of his father and brother, matriculating at Harvard and becoming a lawyer. He inherited his father's Bipolar Disorder, drank excessively and shamed the family with a number of sordid extramarital affairs. True to his name-calling nature and lack of compassion, John Adams once called his son,

> "a madman possessed of the Devil."

Charles died at the age of 30. Adams' third son, Thomas Adams was also a Harvard alum, a gambler and an alcoholic who died at age 59.

John Quincy Adams' son, George Washington Adams, like his father appeared to fight hard to preserve his sanity. Also a Harvard graduate, lawyer and politician, he served on the Boston City Council and as a member of the Massachusetts

House of Representatives. Despite his accomplishments, George battled either Major Depression, Bipolar Disorder or both. At the age of 28, it appears he died by suicide. On April 30, 1829, he reportedly jumped off a steamship into the Long Island Sound at 2 am in the morning. The temperature would have been in the low forties (Farenheit) or less. While it is entirely possible that he could have fallen overboard, investigators found his overcoat and hat on deck. According to people who saw him last, he was acting "delusional." His body was recovered a month later. Another son also inherited a set of regrettable struggles. George's younger brother, John Adams II was an alcoholic and failed businessman. He died at age 31.

This family legacy of generational tragedy is hard to fathom today. However, it was not uncommon in the early 1800's. Mental health treatment in America prior to 1820 ranged from non-existent to harsh, medieval methods of control which are now considered barbaric and condemned by modern standards. Few professionals at this time understood the science of mental health and people struggling with psychotic behavior were immediately labeled as morally degenerate or demonically-possessed. The few insane asylums, jails or alms houses that existed during the lifetime of John Adams often engaged in the use of physical restraints for days at a time, beatings, ice baths, questionable drug concoctions and even bloodletting. The goal of these early facilities was to isolate patients and contain their behavior. There was little to no specialized knowledge regarding treatment or therapy.

As a well-educated, influential and financially secure family of the day, it is likely the Adams family wanted to avoid the shame and cruelty of having a namesake in an asylum or other cruel facility. Therefore, as family members began to descend into deep depressions, manic episodes and engaged in self-medication with alcohol, gambling and illicit sex, they focused more on suppressing the newspaper reports of the day and handling incidents as a "family matter."

The history of the John Adams clan clearly illustrates a medical reality that continues to this day. Bipolar Disorder is often passed down genetically but does not have to devastate that lives of those impacted by the condition. By embracing the information available about the condition and seeking treatment, clients can live long, healthy and successful lives.

Additional Courageous Presidents impacted by Bipolar Disorder

Depiction of President Theodore Roosevelt

Depiction of President Lyndon B. Johnson

FORMER PRESIDENTS TEDDY Roosevelt and Lyndon B. Johnson (LBJ) both displayed moderately manic (hypomanic), powerful personalities and this fueled their early successes in life. However, their versions of Bipolar I Disorder were significantly different from John Adams and slightly different from one another. Roosevelt and Johnson both exhibited Bipolar I Disorder that does not necessarily require the experience of Major Depressive episodes. Historical accounts indicate there was significant circumstantial depression in the life of LBJ and less so with Roosevelt. Another difference between the two latter presidents is that the Roosevelt family presented significant evidence of inherited Bipolar genes being passed down to other family members. The historical record does not bear this out for the Johnson family.

For LBJ, the historically intense pressures he faced during his administration may have caused circumstantial depressive episodes. Looking back, he ascended to the presidency as a result of the Kennedy assassination. At the same time, the nation was roiling with racial strife due to segregation and the rise of the Civil Rights Movement. As a deeply intuitive school teacher, legislator and a son of the American South, he rose to the occasion and was able to lead the nation through this period of turmoil. In fact, it was Johnson's unique background and engaging personality which allowed him to successfully address the social and legislative concerns of the day.

Johnson possessed a uniquely personal gravitas which equipped him to meet with Gov. George Wallace in the morning, negotiate with civil rights leader Martin Luther King Jr. in the afternoon and carve out civil rights legislation that passed into law. It was a remarkable achievement and the energy that he may have derived from his disease's hypomania could have contributed to his success. However, the political price he and the nation paid for honoring the constitutional rights of African Americans and other marginalized groups was to watch millions of white Southerners leave the Democratic Party en masse and seek out the Republican Party. This added significantly to Lyndon Johnson's stress, feelings of abandonment and depression.

12

At the same time, Johnson seemed to slowly sink under the weight of the Vietnam conflict. The troop losses, political complexity and mass protests in American cities caused Johnson to descend into despondency, depression and even signs of psychosis.

A depiction of Americans protesting the Vietnam War near the White House

AT LEAST ONE WRITER who disagreed with a Bipolar diagnosis for the president stated that he simply had "a nervous breakdown." This is a credible analysis of his history but is not conclusive. At the end, he was so overwhelmed that he announced he would not seek an additional term in office. After leaving office, Johnson was devastated as he watched much of his work dismantled by the Republican administration of Richard Nixon. He died several years later an emotionally broken, unhealthy man.

In concluding our exploration into the Bipolar Disorders experienced by John Adams, Theodore Roosevelt, and Lyndon B. Johnson, it becomes evident that these remarkable individuals grappled with immense internal struggles. As we reflect upon their lives, it's essential to approach their stories with empathy and understanding, recognizing the complexities of mental health and the profound impact it can have on even the most influential figures in history.

John Adams, with his fierce intellect and unwavering dedication to the principles of democracy, navigated the turbulent waters of his emotional challenges with resilience and determination. Despite the highs and lows he experienced, Adams remained steadfast in his commitment to shaping the young nation, leaving an indelible mark on American history.

Theodore Roosevelt's boundless energy and enthusiasm hid the tumultuous internal battles he faced. His hypomanic episodes contributed to his ambitious pursuits, propelling him to unprecedented levels of leadership and achievement. On the other hand, Roosevelt also grappled with the shadows of depression, a reminder of the fragility that lies beneath even the most robust facades.

Lyndon B. Johnson's complex personality and formidable political prowess were intertwined with the tumultuous swings of his Bipolar Disorder. As he navigated the corridors of power, Johnson's highs propelled him to bold action, while his lows plunged him into despair. Yet, through it all he remained dedicated to his vision of a Great Society, leaving a legacy that continues to shape society by implementing programs such as Medicare and Medicaid. More specifically, he enacted legislation for American civil rights on behalf of people with disabilities, the LGBTQ community and others who benefit from the gains made on behalf of cultural minorities.

In honoring the legacies of these accomplished presidents, it is important to reflect upon the challenges they faced and the resilience they demonstrated in the face of adversity. By shining a light on their struggles, we not only humanize these historical figures but also foster greater empathy and understanding for those who continue to grapple with mental health challenges today.

Chapter Two: Major Depressive Disorder

When you come out of the grips of a depression, there is an incredible relief but not one you feel allowed to celebrate. Instead, the feeling of victory is replaced with [the] anxiety that it will happen again. [You feel a sense of] shame and vulnerability when you see how your illness [has] affected your family, your work, [and] everything left untouched while you struggled to survive.

- Jenny Lawson, author of <u>Furiously Happy: A Funny Book about Horrible Things</u>

Introduction

THROUGHOUT AMERICAN history, the Oval Office have been occupied by individuals possessed with unparalleled influence and power, shaping the destiny of our nation. Yet, behind the surface of authority and prestige lies a deeply human reality - a reality frequently interrupted by the shadow of Major Depressive Disorder (MDD). Like many other Americans, our presidents have not been immune to its painful and debilitating effects. In both the halls of power and the privacy of the official residence, several former presidents have grappled under the weight of this debilitating illness. In our examination of Major Depressive Disorder in former American presidents, we will summarize in layman terms the elements of the disease and profile the life of an executive who suffered from its impact. Lastly, we will identify several other former executives throughout our nations's history who were impacted by Major Depression Disorder.

Diagnostic Summary

MAJOR DEPRESSIVE DISORDER a mental health condition where a person feels sad or down most of the time, and it affects how they think, feel, and handle daily activities. It's more than just feeling sad because of a bad day or something not going your way. With clinical depression, those feelings can stick around for a long time - weeks or even months. Additionally, people suffering from Major Depression can lose interest in things they used to enjoy, have changes in appetite or sleep patterns, feel tired or have low energy all the time. They might also have trouble concentrating or making decisions. The loss of energy and the interruption of decision-making capabilities can have a devastating impact on a president tasked with leading a nation in which problems and policy decisions are always demanding attention.

There is no single cause of Major Depression. It is frequently a combination of factors such as:

- Genetics (meaning it runs in families);

- brain chemistry (imbalances in certain chemicals that affect mood);

- painful life conditions which may contribute to ongoing, complex trauma;

- Post Traumatic Stress Syndrome (or PTSD) (i.e. shocking events).

The good news is that clinical depression can be treated! There are different ways to help manage it, like therapy where you talk to someone about how you're feeling, learn coping skills, or receive medication that can help balance those chemicals in the brain. Sometimes a combination of therapy and medication works best.

A Presidential Profile - Abraham Lincoln

A depiction of President Abraham Lincoln (circa 1863)

ONE OF THE TERMS MOST frequently associated with Abraham Lincoln during his lifetime was "melancholy," meaning sad or gloomy. Historians report the people closest to our 16th president were generally supportive of him during those periods when he was experiencing low ebbs in his emotional condition. When his feelings descended to deeply alarming levels, friends and family members rallied around him and conducted loosely organized suicide watches to ensure that Abe did not hurt himself. Before being elected to the White House, people took him into their homes for long stretches, removed razors and guns from his home and muttered about feeling powerless to do anything more to help him. Nevertheless, during those occasions when he felt he was reaching a low point, Lincoln was known to take his gun and go on long walks in the woods. He would spend countless hours in solitude and isolation. Fortunately, he returned home safely each time. In describing himself, Lincoln stated,

> "I am now the most miserable man living. If what I feel were equally distributed to the whole human family, there would not be one cheerful face on the earth. Whether I shall ever be better I can not tell; I awfully forebode [predict] I shall not. [Jan 23, 1841]

His Childhood

LIKE MANY PEOPLE WHO lived during his period in the nation's history, Abe Lincoln grew up poor in a hardworking family of laborers who valued grit and long hours working with their hands. His father was openly hostile to the luxuries of study, knowledge and higher education. His father Thomas Lincoln's upbringing convinced him that only common sense and hard work put food on the table, not "book learnin'." When the intellectually curious Abraham would sneak off with a book or a newspaper he found, he often paid for it with a beating from his father. Despite the trauma of ongoing abuse, young Abraham persisted in reading any worthwhile material he could get his hands on.

An even greater challenge to the future president was a multi-generational history of mental illness in his family. Both of his parents exhibited sadness frequently, and his father was described as having "strange spells" during which he would wander off and isolate himself as much as he could during these periods. Several relatives on Tom Lincoln's extended side of the family also showed signs of what could possibly be diagnosed as clinical depression. So pervasive were these family traits, one neighbor who knew the Lincoln clan well quipped that they often displayed "the Lincoln characteristics - moody spells and a great sense of humor!" Another relative descending from Mordecai Lincoln (Abe's uncle and Tom's brother) morbidly described his own mental health challenges as "the Lincoln horrors."

The young Abe Lincoln also experienced a few personal tragedies that certainly exacerbated his inherited tendencies. When his mother Nancy Hanks Lincoln gave birth to Abe's younger brother, Thomas Jr, he was stillborn. Nancy and two other relatives later passed away when he was nine years old from an infectious disease known at the time as "river sickness" or "milk sick." In contemporary terms, it is speculated they succumbed to Tuberculosis. This was particularly painful for Nancy's young son, not only because he regarded his mother as "kind" but also because she shared his tendencies toward intellectual pursuit. When she passed, Abe lost the one family member who truly understood his passion for reading, discovery and discourse.

Lincoln would also endure the painful death of his older sister Sarah. Sarah's death hit him particularly hard as she was close to him. A family member described tears running between his fingers as he buried his face in his hands and sobbed at her deathbed. Despite multiple family losses, poverty and abuse during his formative years, the future president did not exhibit classic signs of Major Depression until later in life.

Around age 24, Lincoln was appointed as postmaster of New Salem, Illinois. Things were looking up and he began a relationship shrouded in mystery with a young woman named Anna Mayes Rutledge. There has been a lot of speculation over the years by historians as to the true nature of their involvement and the real reasons for his decline around the time of her death. Nevertheless, writers and psychobiologists point to Anna's death followed by the immediate onset of cold, wet weather as two precipitating factors that sent young Abe Lincoln reeling. The emotional crash he experienced was documented by family members and may have been the first of two clinically serious breakdowns in his life.

He would experience another mental health episode following a breakup with his future wife, Mary Todd Lincoln. Although they would go on to reconcile, their initial breakup followed by cold, dreary weather overwhelmed Lincoln and he suffered what many consider to be his second serious clinical episode. It was reported that he was deeply depressed and openly made comments about taking his own life.

———————

The Moral Treatment Era of Mental Health in America

LINCOLN LIVED DURING a period in American history in which physicians, religious leaders and other professionals began to approach serious social conditions from a humanitarian approach. In short, the ideas of the Moral Treatment Era were born from the philosophy that by changing a person's physical and social conditions, improvements could be made to their mental, moral and economic living conditions. Asylums and other facilities attempted to abandon imprisonment and control-based approaches to providing safe, restful environments in which people could heal and find their way back to sanity. It was during this period (1845) the word "psychosis" began to appear in medical journals and other writings. Despite their best efforts, the rapid changes the country was undergoing worked against the goals of reformers like Dorthea Dix and physicians of the period. Industrialization, mass immigration of impoverished populations and swelling urban centers all put immense pressure on crowded public mental health asylums and these underfunded facilities were forced to return to basic containment and control mechanisms. The conditions were better than the pre-1820 practices but it would be decades before care improved appreciably, particularly for public institutions. Community-based treatment was still 100 years away as a nationwide concept. Precious few could afford the scarce private treatment services available and practices remained underdeveloped and largely ineffective for serious psychological impairment.

———————

The Lincoln Presidency

WHILE LINCOLN WOULD go on to become one of the most impactful presidents in American history, he continued to struggle with Major Depression throughout his life. He was described by those who knew and worked with him during his political career to be highly disciplined. He religiously maintained structured calendars, daily schedules and learned to manage his emotions despite the onslaught of suicidal ideations and feelings of despair. The American Civil War presented immense challenges to Lincoln and his emotional well-being. Once during a particularly disappointing loss at the Second Battle of Bull Run, the Union Army lost over 13,000 soldiers compared to 8,000+ Confederate losses. One historian, David H. Donald recorded that a despondent President Lincoln admitted during a Cabinet meeting that he felt like hanging himself.

A depiction of President Abraham Lincoln conferring with Abolitionist
Frederick Douglass

ON A LIGHTER NOTE, it has been speculated by some historians that
Lincoln's struggle with mental illness may have curated within him a heightened
sense of compassion and contributed to a softened heart toward the plight of
African American slaves. Conversely, others wrote that it was not compassion
but simply a fear of losing his second election. Nevertheless, with years of
conversations with abolitionists Frederick Douglass, Harriet Beecher Stowe and

others the president's position evolved on the issue. The President and Douglass eventually reached the consensus that maintaining the Union alone could not justify the carnage of the conflict which was ripping the nation apart. They concluded the abolition of American slavery must be on the table as well.

Months later, Abraham Lincoln would be assassinated at Ford's Theatre. Upon her husband's death, Mary Lincoln presented Frederick Douglass with the president's favorite walking cane in recognition of the friendship and political accomplishments of the two men. We may never know the full impact in which Lincoln's personal struggle with Major Depression may have contributed to the Union victory and the abolition of "America's peculiar institution," that of chattel slavery.

Additional Courageous Presidents impacted by Major Depressive Disorder

Depiction of President Woodrow Wilson

IN ADDITION TO ABRAHAM Lincoln, there is no doubt that Major Depressive Disorder has had a direct impact on the historical outcomes of other administrations. The record is replete with other courageous U.S. Presidents who were impacted by this debilitating disease. They include James Madison, John Quincy Adams, Franklin Pierce, Rutherford B. Hayes and James Garfield. During certain periods of his term in office, President Woodrow Wilson was so immobilized by Major Depression that his wife Edith took over the daily activities of the Oval Office. As a result, cynical reporters of the day described his administration as "government by petticoat!" Herbert Hoover and Dwight Eisenhower are also included in a long list of American presidents adversely impacted by Major Depressive Disorder.

A Brief Discussion About Prolonged Grief Disorder

IN MARCH 2022, THE American Psychiatric Association (APA) released an updated version of the Diagnostic Statistical Manual of Mental Health Disorders (DSM) which included for the first time the diagnosis of Prolonged Grief Disorder (PGD). This diagnosis is frequently confused with Major Depressive Disorder because the two disorders share similar characteristics. However, Prolonged Grief Disorder is not the same condition as normal grief, Major Depression, or Post Traumatic Stress Disorder (PTSD).

The APA describes PGD as a "persistent, enduring and disabling grief." Adults who have spent more than a year (six months for children) grieving the loss of a loved one often complain that life has lost all meaning; that a part of them died with the loss; they feel emotionally numb or conversely, they are racked with intense anger or bitterness. The grieving persons may also experience difficulty with planning, inability to re-engage their careers and trouble with pre-existing relationships. Consider the case of former President Coolidge.

A depiction of President Calvin Coolidge

IN JULY 1924, CALVIN Coolidge Jr., the young son of the president by the same name fell ill and died of blood poisoning. A despondent President Coolidge lapsed into a state of administrative paralysis and was reported to have neglected his responsibilities as the nation faced a runup to the 1929 crash on Wall Street. As a rudderless Congress contemplated legislation to rein in rampant stock speculation, President Coolidge told reporters:

> "I have no information relative to proposed legislation about loans on securities. I saw by the press that there was a bill pending in the House or the Senate. I don't know what it is or what its provisions are or what the discussion has been."

Apparently his grief and depression regarding his son rendered him so incapable of formulating a political talking point, he haplessly answered with the truth. Writing in his autobiography, Coolidge sadly reflected,

> " . . . when Calvin Jr. went, the power and glory of the presidency went with him."

Prolonged Grief Disorder can coexist with Major Depression or PTSD in the life of a grieving person. It is critical to understand that only a trained counselor or therapist can accurately distinguish and diagnose these difficult conditions and assist someone in the process of moving beyond persistent grief.

In our discussion of American presidents who struggled with Major Depressive Disorder, we realize the intersection of mental health and presidential history sheds light on the complexity of leadership. Through a thoughtful examination of the lives of these leaders, it becomes apparent that the burden of Major Depressive Disorder can weigh heavily on even the highest office holders in the land. Their struggles offer each of us a reminder that vulnerability and strength are not mutually exclusive. In other words, the pursuit of power and the journey to healing are both integral to the human experience. As we continue to explore the legacies of American presidents, may we honor their humanity and resilience. It is important to recognize that behind every presidency lies a story of courage and in some cases, triumph over adversity, even in the shadow of severe mental illness.

Chapter Three: Narcissistic Personality Disorder

"With all the power that a President has, the most important thing to bear in mind is this: You must not give power to a man unless, above everything else, he has character. Character is the most important qualification the President of the United States can have."

- Richard M. Nixon

Introduction

AS WE CONTINUE OUR discussion on some of the mental health challenges of former American presidents, we will tackle one of the most interesting yet misunderstood mental health diagnoses. Narcissistic Personality Disorder is defined in the Diagnostic and Statistical Manual of Mental Disorders (DSM), the evolving text on American mental health. However, over the years, the word "narcissist" has descended from a medical term into the social media swirl of pejorative language. Many times, it is loosely used to describe anyone who makes us uncomfortable or challenges the status quo. Consequently, it remains that beyond the medical and social work professions, many people do not understand the condition. They are usually unable to define it and their casual banter can do immense harm to the efforts of psychological professionals working furiously to address it and offer help to the people suffering from the condition.

Diagnostic Summary

NARCISSISTIC PERSONALITY Disorder is a mental health condition characterized by an inflated sense of self-importance, a constant need for admiration, and a lack of empathy for others. People with this medical condition often believe they are superior to others, have grandiose fantasies of success and power, and expect special treatment. Despite appearing confident, they often have fragile self-esteem and can be sensitive to criticism. This condition is frequently the result of complex trauma during childhood and other complicating factors in a person's life.

It has been observed by many mental health practitioners there are two observable dimensions to Narcissistic Personalities, a "bright side" or grandiose dimension; and a "dark side" clinically referred to as the vulnerable dimension. Most people and family members see the public side of the disorder: the extroverted persona on display, elevated self-esteem, unethical behavior and a general sense of "disagreeable-ness." The private side is often overlooked or hidden. It is characterized by personal distress, neuroticism, suicidal thoughts / ideation and a tendency to internalize symptoms. The personal aggravation that is often inflicted on people who come in contact with narcissists frequently results in conflict, poor interpersonal relationships and a lack of empathy for what they may be experiencing internally. However, as the general public becomes more aware of the vulnerable experiences that narcissists often suffer there may be an opportunity for more people to demonstrate empathy and compassion toward those burdened with the disorder.

A Presidential Profile - Andrew Jackson

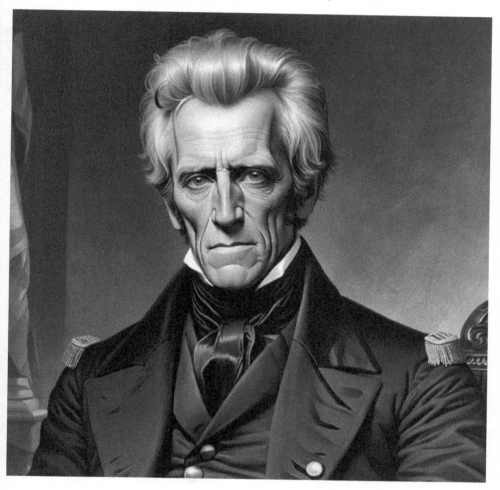

A depiction of President Andrew Jackson (circa 1830)

ANDREW JACKSON, THE seventh President of the United States, is most remembered for his contributions to the expansion of the nation's land out west and for his victories on the battlefield. The importance of Jackson's victory at New Orleans cannot be overstated - it was the turning point in the War of 1812. However, despite his accomplishments Jackson possessed a stormy and violent disposition and at times suffered from severe mental illness and emotional distress. Historians, writers and analysts have suggested Andrew Jackson displayed traits consistent with Narcissistic Personality Disorder and other disorders. He exhibited a sense of self-importance and entitlement, was preoccupied with exercising power, attaining success at all costs, and required excessive admiration by people subordinate to him. He also had a habit of exploiting other people and demonstrated a shocking lack of empathy for others throughout his life. His well-documented inability to control his temper (referred to as emotional dysregulation) probably contributed to the death of at least one man in a duel. More infamously, Jackson is remembered for unspeakable cruelty and neglect toward Native Americans. Thousands perished as a direct result of his actions in the field and policies in the White House.

Jackson's Childhood Trauma

JACKSON WAS NICKNAMED "Old Hickory" as a testament to his physical toughness, wiry frame and explosive temper. As the youngest son in a family of common laborers, Jackson entered this world under tragic circumstances in the years leading up to the Revolutionary War. During the third trimester of his mother Elizabeth Jackson's pregnancy, his father (also named Andrew) was killed in a Carolina logging accident. The family was devastated by the death of their husband and father. While infant Andrew survived physically, he certainly experienced prenatal stress as a result of the toxic hormonal environment induced by his mother's shock, grief and turmoil. These types of experiences are known to place infants at risk for emotional problems, ADHD and lifelong behavioral issues. Prenatal stress can also result in changes to vulnerable infant brain structures and result in impaired cognitive development. Consequently, the death of his father prior to his own birth would be the first step in a debilitating pattern of trauma and loss throughout his childhood, early adult years and into his presidency.

At age 12, Andrew watched as his big brother Hugh left home to serve with the American patriots during the Revolutionary War. Following the Battle of Stono Ferry in June 1779, Hugh died of heat exhaustion. Caught up in the fervor of wartime, Andrew and his remaining older brother Robert both followed in Hugh's steps. They enlisted in a local militia group as messengers on horseback, hoping their young ages would allow them to pass through enemy lines without drawing too much attention. They were subsequently captured, beaten and imprisoned by British regular troops. When the boys came home, both were severely malnourished and sick with Smallpox. Robert succumbed to his illness two days later. Andrew lingered and eventually recovered.

After caring for her two boys and burying Robert, Andrew's mother took a job providing nursing care to American prisoners-of-war aboard a British hospital ship in Charleston Harbor during the revolutionary conflict. As a result of the risks she undertook in a filthy, disease-ridden prison ward on water, Elizabeth contracted Cholera and subsequently died. At this point, a strong-willed but emotionally broken Andrew was the only member of his immediate family left alive. Every person he loved was dead by age 14. The prospect of losing both parents and his two older siblings that he looked up to left him fearful, angry, suffering from depression and experiencing severe attachment issues. This repeated cycle of loss and grief certainly impacted his ability to form meaningful and compassionate relationships with others for the rest of his life.

A depiction of practicing attorney Andrew Jackson

AS A YOUNG ADULT, JACKSON'S emotional dysregulation and anger management issues began to reveal themselves more frequently. There are accounts of him engaging in excessive risk-taking behaviors like dueling, gambling, speculative business ventures, and waging quasi-legal military campaigns. As an attorney and Kentucky horse breeder, Jackson frequently allowed his irritable nature and thin skin to get the best of himself. Whenever he felt slighted by a colleague, he would often challenge them to a duel. It is not known how many duels Jackson participated in during his lifetime but historians generally agree it was too many. As a young lawyer, he was once embarrassed in a courtroom by a more experienced attorney. Enraged, Jackson grabbed an old law book laying next to him and scrawled across one of its pages,

"Sir, I challenge you to a duel!"

Some of the most pointed and infuriating insults he endured resulted from a mistake made by his wife Rachel. Apparently, she and Andrew married without having the assurance that her divorce had been finalized. When the news hit the papers that Rachel was actually married to two men at the same time, the insults rolled in and inflamed the rising politician. During an election season, one newspaper brazenly ran an article asking,

"'Ought a convicted adulteress and her paramour husband to be placed in the highest offices of this free and Christian land?'"

A few of Jackson's political rivals wasted no time in hurling jokes and condemnation at the future president. This resulted in at least three duel challenges.

The most infamous incident in which Jackson was actually shot, he broke the rules of dueling etiquette and proceeded to kill Charles Dickinson. His penchant for issuing senseless challenges and subsequent breach of long-standing traditions caused immense damage to Jackson's reputation, however he seemed unmoved by the social and political costs of his actions. This behavior was likely fueled by an inflated sense of indestructibility and immunity to consequences.

As previously stated, the Moral Treatment era of mental health services would not have offered many answers to a man like Andrew Jackson. First, there were very few to no practitioners in the country that had an informed approach on how to treat mental health struggles, especially those diagnoses that were socially-problematic and not involving deep psychosis. Secondly, the concept and definition of narcissism would not be developed for another 80 - 100 years at the time Andrew Jackson assumed the presidency in 1828. Lastly, we know from empirical evidence that narcissists rarely seek treatment on their own volition.

Their sense of invincibility, self-righteousness and insecurity usually does not lead them into periods of self-reflection and the kind of humility associated with seeking treatment.

<hr>

A Tragic Presidency

DESPITE HER PRESBYTERIAN upbringing and religious piety, Rachel Jackson struggled to control her dietary habits, gained weight and habitually smoked cigars. A few days after her husband won the 1828 presidential contest she complained of excruciating pain in her shoulder and breast areas. She died just a few days after the election but before his inauguration. The president-elect was crushed and grieved bitterly over her death. It was another chapter of deep loss in his life and the following state of depression was unrelenting. Although it was clear she died of health complications (possible heart attack), Jackson blamed her passing on his political enemies and vowed he would never forget.

As his administration got underway, Jackson continued to demonstrate a lack emotional regulation and disturbingly disproportionate responses to provocations or disappointments. In fact, several historians have remarked that Jackson seemed possessed during his eight year long administration with only two goals: revenge against political foes and Indian displacement from Middle America. In one famous example of petty revenge, it was alleged he had his vice presidents' family dogs killed as an act of political retaliation. His lifelong grudges and vendettas suggest severe problems with impulse control.

By a long measure, one of America's greatest self-inflicted wounds was a direct result of Jackson's complete lack of empathy for those he condescended to most - Native Americans. The enactment of the Indian Removal Act by Jackson (his only major piece of legislation in two terms of office) and the execution of its policies under the Van Buren administration was by all measures horrific in practice. The Trail of Tears death march for 60,000 souls nearly stands alone as one of the worst human atrocities in American history. Many historians and psychobiographers believe the depth of cruelty and neglect which led to the deaths of thousands of First Americans was a direct result of a deeply disturbed man reliving or re-enacting violent memories and losses suffered in his own life.

Additional Courageous Presidents impacted by Narcissistic Personality Disorder

THROUGHOUT HISTORY, several other US presidents have displayed traits consistent with clinical narcissism. They include but are not limited to:

John Adams

Andrew Johnson

Lyndon B. Johnson

Richard M. Nixon

Due to the possibility these executives may have suffered from multiple disorders including Narcissistic Personality Disorder, each of them are discussed in greater length in other chapters of this book.

Narcissism can be a difficult illness to diagnose and is often exhibited as a comorbidity (additional disease) along with other challenges such as Major Depression, Bipolar Disorder, PTSD, chemical dependency and other mental health struggles. It also defies accurate diagnosis given that people with narcissism, psychopathy or other dark personality disorders seem to garner either excessive personal support or conversely, very little empathy from the people around them. This is particularly true regarding those who are hurt by their behavior. This creates a great deal of social, political and personal unrest in and around the life of the patient and clouds opportunities for objective observation and clinical diagnosis. This has always been the case throughout history and continues until today.

Chapter Four: Post Traumatic Stress Disorder (PTSD)

―――

"PTSD is a whole-body tragedy, an integral human event of enormous proportions with massive repercussions."

- Susan Pease Banitt

―――

Introduction

THE CONCEPT THAT WE now refer to as Post Traumatic Stress has been observed but rarely understood for thousands of years. The ancient Greek historian Herodotus documented a soldier who witnessed his friend brutally killed in battle. Consequently, the man went blind despite not having any physical damage to his eyes. During America's Industrial Age, the phrase "railway spine" began to circulate as coworkers noticed debilitating symptoms in fellow train and rail yard employees who witnessed terrible accidents. In World War I, soldiers used the term "shell-shocked," and in WWII the term evolved into "battle fatigue" or "combat fatigue."

The Vietnam War was a turning point. Many veterans returned with severe psychological problems. This time, there was more public awareness and media attention. Research expanded beyond combat veterans and began to study survivors of other types of trauma such as sexual assault, police misconduct, child abuse, natural disasters and serious accidents. This broadened our understanding and showed that PTSD could affect anyone who experienced a traumatic event, not just soldiers. As a result, our understanding of PTSD is now based on many years of observation, research, and improvements in medical and psychological science. This knowledge helps us better support and treat individuals affected by traumatic experiences.

Diagnostic Summary

Imagine you go through something really scary or upsetting like a car accident, a natural disaster, or even something like being bullied. This kind of event is called a "traumatic" event because it's really stressful and scary. For most people after something scary happens, they might feel upset for a while but then they start to feel better as time goes on. But for some people, the memory of that scary event sticks around and continues to bother them a lot. This is what we call Post Traumatic Stress Disorder, or PTSD.

People with PTSD might have a hard time forgetting the scary event. They might have bad dreams about it or feel like they're reliving it even when they're awake. Sometimes, they might try really hard to avoid anything that reminds them of what happened because it makes them feel upset all over again. They might also feel jumpy, like they're always on the lookout for danger even when they're safe. This can make it hard for them to concentrate, sleep, or even feel happy.

Think of it like this: When you get a cut on your skin, it usually heals after a while. But sometimes, a cut can leave a scar that stays with you. PTSD is like a scar on your mind from some negative event that happened. It's a way your brain tries to protect you, but it can make things tough because it keeps reminding you of the bad event even when you want to move on. People with PTSD can get help from therapists or counselors who are trained to help them feel better and learn how to deal with these memories in a healthier way.

A depiction of President Franklin Pierce (circa 1855)

WHEN MOST AMERICANS are asked to give the names of U.S. presidents they can remember, Franklin Pierce is frequently one of the names that is either forgotten or never learned in school. Although he was born into a stable, middle-class environment and married into a better family than his own, Pierce became one of those politicians who had a habit of squandering historical opportunity time and again as he rose through the ranks of power and influence. He was a deeply unpopular, one-term president who endured being sacked by his own party after four years. Either as a consequence of mental illness or poor executive management, he managed to produce enemies on both sides of the political aisle and from each half of the Mason-Dixon Line (North and South). Franklin Pierce is one of those leaders that should be remembered and taught more frequently in American history for this simple reason: his most important presidential policies and actions were immensely consequential - for all the wrong reasons.

Early Political Life

THE LIFE OF A POLITICIAN in Washington, D.C. during the 1830s and '40s was a mix of crude living conditions and a boisterous, unruly social environment. A congressman's daily routines were centered around their duties in the legislature, with sessions running from December to March. They spent much of their day in debates, committee meetings and other legislative activities. Nevertheless, a culture of drinking and wild living was integral to the political and social fabric of the time, influencing relationships, decision-making and the overall atmosphere of the nation's capital.

Most legislators in the House and Senate did not own homes in Washington City as it was called at the time. Many of them left their families back home among their constituents and made long, grueling trips by train or stage coach to and from the District of Columbia. They often lived in old boarding houses and clapboard hotels with other members of their same parties. These communal living conditions served as a means of cementing political relationships, learning about other parts of the country and finding interesting ways to pass the time.

For those in temperance (non-drinking) circles and introverted types, time was spent reading, writing and ruminating about missing their loved ones. For those more colorful individuals, the District provided an abundance of opportunities for socializing, hobnobbing with political and social elites like Dolly Madison, Henry Clay, John Calhoun and Daniel Webster. It was also a prime opportunity to meet and be seen with foreign diplomats, wealthy lobbyists and influencers.

As you can imagine, politicians of the era also frequently engaged in heavy drinking, visiting alley-way bordellos and not uncommonly, getting into inebriated arguments and fist fights! It was in this environment that Congressman and later Senator Franklin Pierce learned to drink long into the night and gained a reputation as a rabble-rouser. During his years in the Senate, some of his political opponents branded him as,

"[the] hero of a well-fought bottle."

It was also reported that during these early political years he also began to exhibit signs of depression. In the book, *Life of Franklin Pierce* (1852) one of his closest allies and friends, Nathaniel Hawthorne described the legislator as,

"a young man vigorous enough to overcome the momentary depression."

We now know from mental health research and empirical evidence there is an insidious and often cyclical relationship between heaving drinking and depression. Both conditions seem to worsen the effects of the other and millions of people often find themselves in an uncontrollable cycle of bouncing back and forth between the two. This may have been the case for a young Franklin Pierce.

In terms of his productivity as a legislator, history records that Senator Franklin Pierce accomplished little. It was at this point that the contradictions in his life began to make more political enemies than friends. To start with, Pierce was born and raised in New Hampshire. Despite his Northern roots, young Franklin was pro-Southern in his leanings and appeared to be a staunch advocate of Andrew Jackson in terms of policy. So closely aligned with the 6th president's notions about government, Pierce earned the nickname, "Young Hickory of the Granite Hills."

One of his closest friends and political allies was none other than Jefferson Davis, the future president of the Confederacy. The two men probably first met while serving in the U.S. Senate. This was the environment in which Pierce demonstrated his opposition to the northern abolitionist movement and developed a pro-slavery stance.

A depiction of General Franklin Pierce

AFTER HIS TIME IN THE Senate, the two men would both later serve in the Mexican-American War (1846-48) in which the U.S. forcefully took control of and annexed what is now the State of Texas.

A Tragic Start to a Broken Presidency

WHEN FRANKLIN PIERCE resigned from the Senate in 1841 and moved back to New Hampshire, he assured his wife Jane that he no longer harbored any ambitions for political office and would never return to Washington again. Jane despised the debauchery of Washington and the complexities that political life had imposed on their lives. She frequently chose to live away from the bustle of Washington City during her husband's legislative career, but was well aware of his bouts with heavy drinking and depression. This same pattern of alcoholism and emotional instability was also repeated when he participated in the Mexican-American War. After the war was concluded and Pierce came home, she was satisfied that their lives would settle down in New Hampshire and they would find some semblance of peace and sobriety.

Pres. Franklin Pierce negative [between 1855 and 1865]. Library of Congress.

WHEN THE NATION BEGAN its search for a leader in the upcoming 1852 presidential election, it seemed there were no good candidates on the horizon. The questions of America's "peculiar institution" (chattel slavery) and maintaining the balance of pro-slavery versus anti-slavery states were the big, looming issues facing a divided nation. However, the most prominent politicians of the day were well-known for their positions on the issues and no one seemed to be able to wrangle the two-thirds votes needed to secure their party's nomination. What was needed to appease both sides of the sectional debate was a compromise candidate who would assure each side that their concerns would be taken seriously. It became increasingly clear that the Democrats needed a "dark-horse" candidate that would be acceptable to multiple perspectives.

After dozens of votes, the New Hampshire delegation realized a Northern-born man with Southern sympathies would be a perfect solution. They began working the convention floor, submitted Pierce's name and he quickly became the consensus candidate. Despite accusations of cowardice in battle (the nickname "Fainting Frank" was mentioned more than once) and veterans of the war recalling a reputation for drunkenness in the field, Pierce won the nomination. When Jane heard that he had become the Democratic nominee, she literally passed out from shock and disappointment. Their marriage had been battered by his decades of excessive imbibing, depression and the childhood deaths of their two older sons. Devastated by the news, Jane confronted her husband and accused him of lying about his ambitions for higher office. The only bright spot in the Pierce household was their youngest son Bennie, now 10 or 11 years of age. Despite Pierce's lack of a strong legislative record and low national visibility, he won the election of 1852. Jane swallowed her anger and prepared herself to grudgingly return to Washington.

Falling Into the Abyss

Two months prior to his 1853 Inauguration as President of the United States, the Pierce family traveled to Boston to attend the funeral of Jane's uncle. As Franklin, Jane and Bennie made their way back to Concord, New Hampshire by rail, the train lurched violently and then derailed off its tracks. As the wood-framed car descended down an embankment, they began to break apart and chaos ensured. When the splintered wood and glass stopped flying and the broken rail car settled in place, a shocked and dazed Franklin looked at his wife and realized she was bruised but alive. He then turned around to see Bennie who was seated behind them. It is historically unclear whether the young boy was still within the car or was thrown clear. However, when Franklin found Bennie and removed his cap, he was horrified to see that not only was his only remaining son dead, but was nearly decapitated. It was January 6, 1853. The President-elect and his wife experienced a psychological trauma from which neither parent ever recovered from.

The administration of Franklin Pierce was nearly destroyed before it ever began. While he would go on to assume office, the Post Traumatic Stress of the train accident worsened his battles with depression, pushed him to self-medicate with alcohol and inflamed his worst inner tendencies with regard to slavery and compassion for vulnerable people. He had never been a strong leader as a congressman and now, his ability to lead was even more compromised. Journalists and observers of the period recall that Jane withdrew from public life for nearly his entire administration. They described her as "ghostly" in her appearance and she remained emotionally vacant for the rest of her life.

Initially, there was an incredible outpouring of support across the nation for the grieving President and his family. However, the country was deeply divided along sectional lines with regard to managing regional conflicts and Pierce seemed to make poor decisions regarding this challenge at every turn. Rather than promoting and signing legislation that cooled the extreme rhetoric and offered compromise to all parties involved, Pierce advocated for and signed the Kansas-Nebraska Act. With the stroke of a pen, he ripped the Missouri Compromise to pieces which had kept the peace for years. Specifically, he disabled a series of laws that kept a lid on the slavery question for decades and sent the Kansas/Missouri territories into chaos.

The rush of white settlers into this area was not merely motivated by families looking for property to build on but was fueled by pro- and anti-slavery partisans who now held the power to change the balance of the nation. By seizing land and establishing homesteads, they feverishly voted to secure each future state's status as either free or enslaved. So violent was the killing and the imprisonment of combatants by rogue sheriffs, the period became known as "Bloody Kansas." This catastrophic misstep by a president tasked with bringing healing and compromise to the nation caused Pierce to lose friends and support from among both Northerners and Southerners.

In 1854, another historic confrontation played out in Boston. A man named Anthony Burns escaped from his enslaver, Charles Suttle in Virginia. He made his way to Boston, a city known for its support for the abolition of slavery. When Suttle learned that Burns was spotted in Massachusetts, he filed charges and had Burns arrested under what was known as the Fugitive Slave Act of 1850.

A depiction of a free Anthony Burns living in Boston

PEOPLE IN BOSTON FILLED the streets in protest over Burns' arrest. Word of the conflict made national headlines and both sides appealed to Washington to accept their arguments. Despite his long-standing position to not commit federal resources to solve local and state challenges, President Pierce acted on his Southern tendencies and sent active duty Army soldiers to escort Burns back to Virginia. A local magistrate ordered Burns to be handed over to the government and he was returned to Virginia by ship transport under federal guard.

Burns was later freed from bondage when Northerners raised enough money to purchase his freedom. However, the spectacle drew widespread condemnation

50

throughout the country and was seen as a blatant display of federal power supporting the institution of slavery. Once again, Pierce failed to calm sectional fears and managed to lose Northern support despite his New Hampshire roots. His actions in the Anthony Burns case haplessly pushed the nation closer to Civil War. This was another self-inflicted wound on a president steeped in depression, drinking heavily and burdened with a historically consequential period in American history.

As if Pierce could not fail the nation even more, another opportunity for positive change slipped through his fingers and the nation found itself in worse straits as a result. Mental health institutions in America in the 1850's were often little more than filthy, abusive prisons, underfunded and burdened with immense shame and stigma. The conditions of these facilities meant patients were shuttled off to distant locations, locked up and often forgotten by families who were too poor or unwilling to provide adequate care for their afflicted kin. For others who were not institutionalized, they frequently found themselves homeless, hungry and exploited by a population that had little understanding of brain disease, mental illness and complex trauma.

During the Pierce administration, the Congress was lobbied tirelessly by a Massachusetts school teacher and mental health advocate named Dorothea Dix. As a veteran in the field who had helped to organize and bring compassionate care to 30+ institutions at the state and local level, Dix found a congressional sponsor for her advocacy. She wrote a national proposal for a "Bill for the Benefit of the Indigent Insane." The bill aimed to allocate federal land to be sold, with the proceeds used to fund mental hospitals and care for the indigent insane (as was the term in her day). The bill was passed by Congress and sent to the desk of Franklin Pierce.

It would stand to reason that a man who had endured his own severe bouts of depression, alcoholism and post traumatic stress with the deaths of all three of his children would have understood the compelling nature of the legislation sitting before him. Instead of becoming a champion for the bill and setting a national precedent for the care of vulnerable citizens, President Pierce vetoed the legislation in May 1854. He cited his aversion to using federal resources to solve local and state problems. His actions that day dripped with hypocrisy and national regret. The same president that sent federal troops to escort a single escaped bondsman in chains from Boston back to Virginia refused to allow the sale of excess federal land to create safe institutions for indigent, mentally ill Americans in their time of need. Dorothea Dix and many members of Congress were shocked and angered by Franklin's insensitivity.

A depiction of an indigent American man in the 1850s

MANY HISTORIANS EXPLAIN his actions as an effort to deny his own struggle and shame. They posit that he did not want to be seen as having any connection to issues regarding mental illness. This callous action on the part of Pierce set a presidential precedent for non-action regarding social causes that lasted decades. It would be nearly 80 years before another American president had the courage to support and pass federal legislation for social welfare and demonstrate compassion for the less fortunate. In the ensuing period from 1854 to the 1930s, untold thousands of Americans suffered and died from untreated mental illness, unsupported disabilities, spousal abuse, homelessness, preventable disease, child exploitation and labor-related abuses during America's Industrial Age.

In summary, President Franklin Pierce's policies and actions led to widespread unpopularity and division within the Democratic Party. Many Northern Democrats were alienated by his pro-Southern stance, while Southern Democrats did not fully trust him either. This lack of a solid support base within his own party made it difficult for him to secure the nomination for a second term and he was summarily dropped from the ticket by his own party. This was at the time and remains a rare rebuke in presidential politics. Overall, his presidency was marked by a lack of leadership due to his preoccupation with grief, alcoholism and bouts of depression. At a time when America desperately needed a president to manage the growing tensions between the North and South, his administration was seen as weak and ineffective. He failed to unify the Democratic Party or the nation at a critical time in the nation's history. He died in 1869 of cirrhosis of the liver, a common cause of death for people suffering from grief, depression, trauma and severe chemical dependency.

Chapter Five: Alcohol Use Disorder

"Whether I or anyone else accepted the concept of alcoholism as a disease didn't matter; what mattered was that when treated as a disease, those who suffered from it were most likely to recover."

- Craig Ferguson, *American on Purpose: The Improbable Adventures of an Unlikely Patriot*

Introduction

TO UNDERSTAND THE IMPACT of alcohol and other substances, we must first realize the brain is a major control center for your body. It sends messages to different parts of your body to do things like move, feel emotions, and think. There are messengers that help or distract your brain while it works to do its job. They include the foods we eat, medicines we take and chemicals we ingest including alcohol, illicit drugs and other substances.

Diagnostic Summary

THE LONG-TERM USE OF substances like alcohol, drugs and certain medications can do immense harm to how the brain and other organs function. These substances can change how your brain works by interfering with bodily messages. More importantly, the brain can begin to depend on these over-used chemicals by carving new neural pathways in existing brain networks. It's like the brain gets used to having these substances around all the time and finds ways to incorporate them into its daily functions.

Now, here's where it gets tricky. When someone's brain gets used to having these substances all the time, they might feel like they can't function normally without them. They begin to crave or need the substance just to feel okay or to get through the day. This causes what is popularly known as addiction or dependency.

A Presidential Profile - Richard Nixon

A depiction of President Richard M. Nixon (circa 1970)

RICHARD M. NIXON IS reported to have grown up as an intelligent but intensely shy young man. Historians report that in his political enthusiasm to draw a distinction between himself and John Kennedy, he occasionally gave the impression he was raised in "log-cabin" circumstances, however this was far from the truth. He may have been raised on the "wrong side of Whittier" (California) but his father provided a moderate living in Southern California, one that was far more fortunate than in many other parts of the country.

It is frequently reported that Nixon's father was "mean-spirited" and his mother emotionally distant. He was raised as a religiously-minded Quaker but religious practices did not protect him from what is known as complex childhood trauma. Nixon was one of several U.S. presidents known to have lost two siblings during his youthful years. Richard was only 13 years of age when brother Arthur died and 20 years of age when Harold Nixon died. Both of the Nixon boys passed away from complications of Tubercular Encephalitis. Research has shown that presidents who lost two siblings and / or other immediate family members during their youth were at significant risk of lifelong complex trauma and attachment issues. Richard Nixon was no exception. These losses left him deeply wounded and insecure. Despite his academic and professional successes, he struggled with basement-level self-esteem and a loathing self-image for the remainder of his life.

While still in high school, young Richard turned down a scholarship to Harvard due to the expenses of living on the East Coast and attended a local college near home. After graduating, he entered the Navy, served his country during WWII and returned home to the life of a small-town lawyer. The prospect of handling real estate transactions and petty divorces must have bored him to tears, so he kept his ear to the ground waiting for better opportunities. In 1946 when the local Republican Party operatives asked him to run against a nearly invincible Democratic incumbent, Nixon jumped at the chance. Always looking to prove himself, the young Republican was a fast learner when it came to playing dirty politics and defeated the five-term congressman for the 12th District in California. He was off to the races and won several other impressive victories over the next two decades.

The Nixon Presidency

IT IS NOT KNOWN WHEN chemical dependency began to be a problem in the Nixon household but it has been widely reported that both he and Pat Nixon struggled with alcohol. He also abused her physically on more than one occasion. As the pressures of political life increased, the future president not only drank heavily but also resorted to pills. In 1968, Jack Dreyfus, author of the book *A Remarkable Medicine Has Been Overlooked*, made the following confession:

> "Nixon said, 'Why don't you give me some Dilantin?' So I thought, 'What the heck, he's [going to be] president of the United States. I can't get in trouble...' So I went out to the car and got a bottle of a thousand and gave it to him."

Jack Dreyfus was NOT a physician and this may have been the beginning of Nixon's terrible dependency on Dilantin, sleeping pills and even amphetamines.

By 1971, Nixon was functioning well in public but his use of alcohol and sleeping pills was escalating. Paranoia began to set in and he ordered the Oval Office and Cabinet Room in the White House to be outfitted with recorders. In the coming months, other government facilities including Camp David also had recorders installed. The President alone was in control of the tapes.

The early months of 1972 appeared to be going well. That year, Nixon would make history as the first sitting U.S. President to visit both China and the Soviet Union. However, the charade of a successful presidency would abruptly vanish. On June 17th of the same year, four of Nixon's operatives were arrested by police for breaking into the Watergate Building, home office of the Democratic National Party. Despite this embarrassing setback, Nixon was re-elected.

As 1973 got underway, the Nixon White House was embroiled in controversy surrounding the break-in. Nixon initially denied any responsibility but later accepted limited responsibility. As the Senate Watergate Committee began drilling into the White House's crumbling story, Vice President Spiro Agnew came under renewed scrutiny for campaign violations and corrupt acts while he was Governor of Maryland. When the Senate Committee demanded the White House tapes, Nixon refused to turn them over and ordered all taping activities to cease.

The administration was experiencing an incredibly stressful year, the president's career was closing in around him and he was running out of answers. By summertime, the high flying president that broke bread with both the Chinese and Soviet leaders that Spring was now drinking heavily during the day and losing his grip on power. Senior staffers were beginning to assume greater responsibility for daily operations and Henry Kissinger was increasingly becoming the lead on American foreign policy. Vietnam raged on and Nixon couldn't cope.

A Depiction of the 4th Arab-Israeli War

IN THE FIRST WEEK OF October 1973, the 4th Arab-Israeli war broke out. On the 10th of that same month, Spiro Agnew resigned the Vice Presidency due to his own troubles. At this point, Nixon was distraught. The next day the British Prime Minister called to consult with the president on the matters unraveling in the Middle East. A compromised and depressed Richard Nixon was too inebriated to accept the call. This was verified by Secretary of State Henry Kissinger and the president's Chief of Staff, Alexander Haig.

Nearly a year later, the U.S. Supreme Court ruled against Nixon and ordered that he turn over 64 White House tapes. Given the damaging content of the tapes, Nixon resigned on August 8, 1974. The next day when Vice President Gerald Ford was sworn in, he stated to the nation,

"My fellow Americans, our long national nightmare is over."

Nixon would go on to be indicted on criminal charges, however he was granted a full pardon by President Ford.

Richard Nixon is one of the few American presidents known to have sought help from a trained mental health professional. His relationship with Dr. Arnold Hutschnecker is well documented and seems to have provided him support, comfort and political advice from as early as the 1950's to 1993 when Pat Nixon was memorialized. To his credit, Dr. Hutschnecker did not discuss his conversations with Nixon during the president's lifetime, but he did offer this bit of sage advice:

"mental health certificates should be required for political leaders, similar to the Wasserman test demanded by states before marriage."

Nixon was fortunate to have lived in a period of American history in which mental health services were well-developed, accessible and effective. It is also notable that despite his failures, President Nixon's greatest legacy may lie in his weaknesses, not in his areas of talent or strength. He displayed courage in allowing himself to absorb the wisdom of a trained mental health professional. There are times when a man's superpower and his greatest vulnerability are the same.

Additional Courageous Presidents impacted by Alcohol Use Disorder

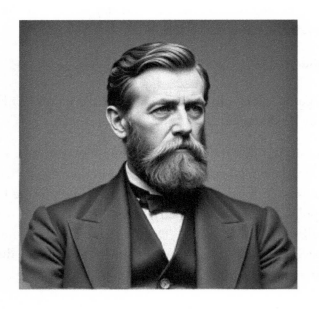

A depiction of President Ulysses S. Grant

THE 18TH PRESIDENT Ulyssess Grant also struggled with alcohol throughout his life. During his initial military career prior to the Civil War, Grant was forced to resign his commission, allegedly for dereliction of duty. In his own words he confessed,

> "the vice of intemperance (drunkenness) had not a little to do with my decision to resign."

Although he joined the Sons of Temperance after his resignation and experienced long periods of sobriety, he would continue to battle the disease of alcoholism.

A Depiction of President Franklin Pierce

PRESIDENT FRANKLIN Pierce began struggling with alcohol as a young politician stationed in Washington, living alone and away from his family. These alcohol-infused tendencies and depression were intensely aggravated after a horrific train accident. He and his wife never recovered from the trauma.

An Additional Courageous President

A depiction of President John F. Kennedy

JOHN KENNEDY'S USE of alcohol and other substances had a notable impact on both his personal life and administration. Kennedy suffered from a range of health problems, including chronic back pain, Addison's disease, and other ailments. To manage his symptoms, he was prescribed various medications, including painkillers and stimulants. Some accounts suggest that he also used alcohol to cope with his medical conditions and the stress of his political career. Kennedy's substance use was generally kept private, and there is limited direct evidence linking it to specific policy decisions. However, his health issues managed through various medications and alcohol might have influenced his performance and stamina during crucial moments.

During his presidency, Kennedy faced significant crises, including the Cuban Missile Crisis and the early stages of the Vietnam War. While his leadership in these situations is often praised for its decisiveness and strategic acumen, the pressures of these events combined with his health challenges could have impacted his stress levels and decision-making processes. Overall, while the direct impact of Kennedy's substance use on his presidency is not fully documented, it cannot be completely discounted or ignored.

The impact of alcoholism on American presidents offers a sobering lens through which to examine the intersection of personal struggles and public leadership. From Ulysses S. Grant's battles with drinking during a critical period of Reconstruction to John F. Kennedy's private reliance on substances amidst Cold War tensions, the influence of alcoholism on presidential decision-making and effectiveness cannot be overlooked. Richard Nixon's tenure was marred by the Watergate scandal and compounded by increasing alcohol use. This illustrates how untreated complex childhood trauma can inflame personal vices and worsen political crises, impair judgment, and diminish one's capacity for effective governance.

This exploration highlights the importance of addressing personal health issues within the broader context of public service. It underscores the need for greater awareness and support systems for those in positions of leadership, ensuring that personal struggles do not unduly compromise their professional responsibilities. Ultimately, understanding the impact of alcoholism on presidential performance offers valuable insights into the broader narrative of leadership, vulnerability, and resilience in the highest office of the land.

Chapter Six: Anxiety Disorder

―――

"I lied and said I was busy.

I was busy;

but not in a way most people understand.

I was busy taking deeper breaths.

I was busy silencing irrational thoughts.

I was busy calming a racing heart.

I was busy telling myself I am okay.

Sometimes, this IS my busy -

and I will not apologize for it."

― Brittin Oakman

―――

Introduction

IN THIS CHAPTER, WE delve into the topic of anxiety as it was experienced by some former United States presidents. From the weight of responsibility to the scrutiny of the press and public opinion, the presidency has been a persistent hotseat that has tested the mental fortitude of those who have held the highest office in the land. Let's examine the personal struggles, coping mechanisms, and historical context surrounding anxiety in some of the most iconic figures in American political history.

―――

Diagnostic Summary

IMAGINE YOU'RE WALKING down a dark alley, and suddenly you hear footsteps behind you. Your heart starts racing, your palms get sweaty, and you feel this overwhelming sense of fear. That's what anxiety feels like. However, instead of just happening in scary situations it can happen at any time. Even when everything seems okay. Anxiety is a lot like having a loud, obnoxious friend who won't stop yelling about potential problems, even when everything is just fine.

It's your brain's alarm system that has become overly sensitive, constantly sending danger signals when there's no real threat. This can make you feel worried, nervous, or even panicky about everyday situations.

A depiction of President / General Ulysses S. Grant (circa 1871)

PRESIDENT AND GENERAL Ulysses S. Grant is a lesson in contrasts. He was one of those individuals that failed miserably in his early career and yet rose to the occasion in spectacular fashion when confronted with chaos, challenge and the horrors of war. Let"s examine the life of a man whose emotional and mental health struggles hid his giftedness for many years of his early life.

The 18th President of the United States was born Hiram Ulysses Grant on April 27, 1822, in Point Pleasant, Ohio. He had a typical mid-19th century American childhood. His father, Jesse Root Grant operated a tannery in their local community and was, by and large a successful businessman. Hannah Simpson Grant was a kind and gentle mother, well-respected for her integrity and generous nature. Young Ulysses was often tasked with working at the tannery as a boy, although it was not his favorite activity. Whenever he could get out of chores at his father's shop, he made beeline for the stables. It did not take long for him to develop a reputation for skilled horsemanship in his boyhood village of Georgetown, situated about 23 miles from his birthplace.

Historians and mental health professionals have speculated that throughout his life, Grant demonstrated several common traits of what is now known as Asperger's Syndrome. He was socially withdrawn in terms of his personal demeanor, and exhibited an uncanny giftedness with horses. It was said he preferred their company instead of people. He also developed an intense ability to focus on tasks, concentrate and grasp minor details that may have escaped others. These skills would later serve the future General and President Grant well. There does not seem to be any record of severe abuse or trauma in his childhood, although he may have been bullied at times due to his slender build and effeminate appearance.

When Ulysses turned 17 years of age, Jesse sensed that his son needed a challenge to help him mature and develop his social skills. He tapped into his business network and spoke with Congressman Thomas Hamer of Ohio. Within short order, the elder Grant secured an appointment for young Ulysses to the United States Military Academy at West Point, New York in 1839. While the shy kid from Georgetown may have initially resisted being thrust out of the security of his boyhood community, the opportunity to escape the drudgery of the tanning business appealed to him and he accepted the opportunity. History records that when Hamer's office registered Ulysses for the academy, an administrative error listed him as Ulysses Simpson Grant as opposed to his actual name, Hiram Ulysses Grant. Whether it was due to the boy's unwillingness to object or his own desire to honor his mother's maiden name, the garbled name stuck and he never changed it again.

Grant at West Point

DURING HIS TRAINING at the nation's military academy, Grant was an average student. He found subjects like engineering and mathematics challenging but managed to maintain decent grades through perseverance, concentration and hard work. The structured and disciplined environment of West Point also helped Grant develop a sense of duty and responsibility. He was not particularly outgoing but was respected by his peers for his honesty and reliability. Despite his moderate academic performance, Grant excelled in the equestrian arts and demonstrated remarkable skill and control when handling horses. To the amazement of his instructors and classmates, he set a high-jump record with his favorite mount that stood for 25 years. The training he received was instrumental in shaping his approach to military leadership.

In addition to a critical skillset in battlefield tactics and commanding soldiers, Grant formed several important friendships during his time at West Point, including with future Civil War generals James Longstreet and William T. Sherman. He also developed a close friendship with Frederick Tracy Dent, brother of his future wife. These connections would prove to be pivotal in his military career and life. Ulysses graduated from West Point on July 1, 1843. His class rank of 21 of 39 was lower than he had hoped, but his performance was respectable given his initial challenges. Upon graduation, Grant was commissioned as a Brevet Second Lieutenant in the 4th U.S. Infantry Regiment. He was assigned to Jefferson Barracks near St. Louis, Missouri, marking the beginning of his professional career as an officer.

Grant's Early Military Service

A YEAR AFTER GRADUATING from the academy, Ulysses and his buddy Frederick Dent traveled to Dent's family plantation. It was there that Ulysses met his wife-to-be Julia Dent. Pious and strong-willed, she became a fierce defender and support system for her husband. Grant's marriage to Julia was one of the most fortuitous decisions in his life given that she served as a solid, stabilizing force throughout his career and beyond. America probably would have never benefited from the career and accomplishments of this Civil War general and Reconstruction president were it not for the hand of Julia Dent Grant in his life. In August 1844, Ulysses and Julia were married at the Dent family estate. The groom was flanked by Frederick, her brother; James Longstreet, her cousin; and a third Westpoint graduate. Unfortunately, Ulysses' parents were avowed abolitionists and refused to attend the ceremony on a plantation holding African Americans in bondage.

History may not have recorded if there were mishaps or traumatic events in Grant's early military career. What we do know is that at some point, the well-trained West Point man known for his riding skills and personal discipline developed a drinking problem. Did he experience something on the battlefield that devastated him? A brush with death, the horrific loss of a buddy close to him? It may be possible that some personal experience harmed him psychologically or that his natural anxiety and introversion caused him to descend into isolation, loneliness and depression. What we do know from ample documentation including his own memoirs is that alcohol was a significant coping mechanism that he used throughout his adult life to manage stress, anxiety and personal pain.

GRANT ENTERED THE MEXICAN War in 1846 as a quartermaster. The role of the quartermaster was vital to the Army's effectiveness, ensuring that soldiers had the supplies and equipment to sustain long campaigns and ultimately achieve victory. Although he distinguished himself more than once in battle, he had to endure constant ribbing from his fellow soldiers. Apparently some of the officers in his regiment called him "Little Beauty," a nickname mocking his slender body type, facial structure and soft voice. According to an early biographer the young man,

> ". . . had a girl's primness of manner and was modest in his behavior. His hands had the long, tapering fingers of a woman. He was almost half-woman."

Grant was also known for his strict food routine with respect to the cooking of meat and an aversion to the sight of blood. This was also attributed to a potential diagnosis of Asperger's Syndrome.

> "I have seen many wounded men in my time, but I never could become reconciled to the sight of blood."

> - Letter to his wife Julia Dent Grant (1847)

Two years later, Ulysses would be transferred to Ft. Humboldt, California and Julia frequently followed her husband to some duty stations as a faithful Army wife. As time went on there were reports that Grant's drinking led to several incidents of intoxication while on duty. This did not go unnoticed by his superiors. His commanding officer, Colonel Robert Buchanan, was particularly critical of Grant's conduct. It is believed that Grant was given a merciful ultimatum by Buchanan to either resign or face a court-martial for his behavior. In military circles, this was a shocking setback for a West Point graduate. Grant chose to resign from the army and submitted his resignation letter on April 11, 1854. The resignation was accepted, and he officially left the service in July 1854.

LIFE AFTER THE ARMY was not a happy time for the quiet, shy man who was suddenly without employment and suffering from a loss of identity. With responsibilities for feeding his family, Grant returned to Missouri near his in-laws farm and tried his hand at tilling the ground and raising crops. Due to his lack of experience and poor soil, his labors were in vain and this put a severe strain on his marriage. The relationship between he and his in-laws was further tested due to the fact that Julia's family were enslavers of black Americans. Grant was opposed to chattel slavery and his unwillingness to used slave labor probably contributed to his failure to get the best results from the land. He left farming and worked as a bill collector and real estate agent in town. Despite his best efforts, he found little success at these occupations as well. Finally, Grant reluctantly decided to return to an industry that he knew well. He moved his family from Missouri to Galena, Illinois in 1860 where his father owned a leather goods store.

A depiction of Grant & Perkins Leather Store, Galena, Illinois

GALENA WAS A BUSTLING and diverse mining town on the Mississippi River in the mid-1800s. It was a hub for a large immigrant population that came to work in the lead mines, trading occupations, and on the docks. Galena was also a great location for a man of Grant's professional background. Not only did it give him a fresh start in a new town, he also became immersed once again in finished leather goods including saddles, harnesses and other supplies. He quickly became manager of the family-owned store as a result of his training in the Army as a quartermaster. His father gave him full reign to improve operations when he realized his son had deep experience in the logistical management of large quantities of durable goods. As the business grew under his watchful eye and accurate bookkeeping skills, their juxtaposition on the river facilitated sales not only to the local farming and mining communities but to other locations up and down the Mississippi. He felt after years of struggling he finally regained a place in an unforgiving economy.

Grant's work in Galena also allowed the emotionally battered husband and father to regain his confidence and self-esteem. He had the space to think about his priorities in life and reduce his stress at the same time. It was a pivotal time for rebuilding his mental health, character and improve his sobriety. He and Julia settled once again into a pleasant relationship, but secession was brewing in the Deep South and the country was on edge. The positive community relationships he developed in Galena and a good reputation were critical to Grant re-entering the Union Army at the commencement of civil hostilities.

Grant's Return To Military Service

THE CIVIL WAR BROKE out in April 1861 with the Confederate attack on Fort Sumter, a federal installation in South Carolina. Grant was eager to serve and help preserve the Union. He was appointed to a position in the Illinois militia. His prior military experience, competence and maturity quickly led to a series of promotions. As an army commander, Grant displayed leadership qualities that set him apart from many of his peers. His ability to lead confidently without being abusive was particularly noted by his enlisted soldiers and junior officers.

Just as critical as his troop leadership skills and horsemanship was the insight gained from years of serving as an Army quartermaster. The role of the quartermaster was vital to the Union Army's effectiveness, ensuring that soldiers had the necessary resources to sustain long campaigns and ultimately achieve victory. This role required Grant to support his fighting units by managing the acquisition and distribution of supplies including clothing, food rations, weapons, ammunition, tents, tools and medical supplies. He also had to become an expert at military supply routes, camp construction, logistics and transportation. Historian Ronald White pointed out in Grant's biography that he mastered the art and science of,

"provisioning a large, mobile army operating in hostile territory."

This expertise became even more valuable years later to the young quartermaster-turned- commander. It taught him that success on the battlefield was dependent on many strategic factors beyond the tactics of firing guns at opposing forces and positioning lines of infantry. He learned those lessons well and was highly effective at integrating that knowledge and experience into his strategies for deploying and managing his forces for the Union during the Civil War.

Nevertheless, his personal vulnerabilities were ever-present with him. As Grant's stress and anxiety intensified, he penned a letter to his friend Simon Buckner in 1861 stating,

"You have no idea how this war is preying upon my mind. I feel sometimes as if I should go wild."

Grant persevered through his personal struggles and achieved national renown for his victories at Forts Henry and Donelson, Shiloh, Vicksburg and Chattanooga in the Western Theatre. In an 1863 letter to Grant, his superior General-in-Chief of the Armies of the United States Henry Halleck stated,

"You are hereby authorized to disregard any orders from Washington which you may think detrimental to your operations. The Government has full confidence in your judgment and patriotism and wishes you to act entirely on your own discretion."

———————————

A depiction of General Ulysses S. Grant commanding troops in the field.

SECRETARY OF WAR EDWIN Stanton also sent a telegram to the celebrated leader on July 3, 1863 after the win at Vicksburg:

> "The thanks of this Department, the Government and the people of the United States, their reverence and honor, have been deserved and will be rendered to you and the brave and gallant officers and soldiers of your army for all time."

Following Chattanooga, President Lincoln felt he had found in Grant the commander with a decisive resolve that other Union generals in the Eastern

Theatre had lacked. After careful thought, the President promoted Grant to overall command of Union armies in March 1864.

"The particulars of your plans I neither know nor seek to know. You are vigilant and self-reliant; and, pleased with this, I wish not to obtrude any constraints or restraints upon you."

- Letter to General Grant from President Lincoln (April 30, 1864)

By the end of the year, Lincoln expressed to the nation his gratitude for the accomplishments of Ulysses Grant. In a message to Congress by President Lincoln on December 6, 1864, he stated,

"The skill and valor of our Generals and soldiers have been worth more than a million of men. While I am deeply grateful for the large measure of success with which Providence has blessed our arms, it gives me special pleasure to acknowledge the almost inestimable services of the General at the head of our armies."

Nevertheless, the high-handed praise of General Grant from Washington City was tempered at times by the concerns of officers under his command who complained about his drinking in both official cables and personal murmuring. Major General Charles F. Smith served with Grant in the field and expressed concerns about Grant's mechanisms for coping with stress. Brigadier General James H. Wilson, who served on Grant's staff also noted instances of Grant's drinking and expressed concern about its effect on his decision-making and behavior. Brigadier General John McClernand who led McClernand's Volunteers, was known to be a politically-minded general who served under Grant and had a contentious relationship with him. He often complained about Grant's habits, partly as a means to undermine his command.

While Secretary of War Stanton generally supported Grant, he was aware of the rumors about Grant's personal behavior and kept a close watch on the situation. Henry Halleck, Grant's military superior in Washington received multiple reports and complaints about Grant's drinking. He initially harbored doubts about Grant's reliability due to these reports, but later supported Grant more firmly as his successes in the field became undeniable. Despite these complaints, President Abraham Lincoln famously defended Grant, valuing his effectiveness as a general above the rumors of his alleged alcoholism. In response to complaints about Grant's drinking, Lincoln confessed,

"I can't spare this man; he fights."

The president's confidence in Grant's abilities ultimately helped ensure that he retained his command and continued to lead the Union Army to crucial victories. In his two-volume set, *The Personal Memoirs of U. S. Grant*, the troubled leader recalled years later:

"The responsibility of command was terrible, and I was fully aware of the weight of it. My anxiety was intense."

Grant's Presidential Administration

AS THE NATION'S MOST popular war hero at the conclusion of the bloodiest conflict in American history, Ulysses Grant rode a wave of goodwill and support all the way to the White House. He distinguished himself from his predecessor Andrew Johnson by continuing the legacy of Lincoln and working to heal a broken nation. He is remembered for successfully developing and managing the Reconstruction process, appointing many African Americans and Jewish Americans to important federal posts, enforcing the 14th and 15th Amendments on behalf of African Americans and implementing the Social Security system.

The details and accomplishments of his two-term administration are mainly positive but history is evolving on the question of the extent to which anxiety and alcoholism played a role in his presidency. A significant number of historians write that alcohol did not play a role in destabilizing his work as Commander In Chief and administrator of the people's business. It is fair to say that his second term was rocked by a series of scandals. Some attribute this to his former habits, however there is no conclusive proof one way or the other. The prevailing view is that while he had a past marred by alcoholism, his drinking was not a dominant factor during his presidency. Instead, his administration's successes and failures were influenced by a range of factors beyond his personal struggles.

What we can deduce from his personal history is that President Grant had a strong ability to adapt, learned from his early career failures and was deeply indebted to the support and guidance of his wife Julia. His White House staff also deserves much credit for understanding his weaknesses. His biographers observed that they were committed to keeping him busy and managing his schedule and travel in ways that minimized his propensity to feel overwhelmed and turn to alcohol.

Bibliography

A history of presidential rages and tantrums, from Adams to Trump. By Gillian Brockell, July 1, 2022. Retrieved from https://www.washingtonpost.com/history/2022/07/01/donald-trump-ketchup-angry-presidents/

Barber, James David. The Presidential Character: Predicting Performance in the White House. 4th ed., Pearson Longman, 2008.

Calhoun, Charles W. The Presidency of Ulysses S. Grant. University Press of Kansas, 2017. JSTOR, https://doi.org/10.2307/j.ctt1w6t9gz . Accessed 23 July 2024.

Davidson JR, Connor KM. The impairment of Presidents Pierce and Coolidge after traumatic bereavement. Compr Psychiatry. 2008 Jul-Aug;49(4):413-9.

Davidson JR, Connor KM, Swartz M. Mental illness in U.S. Presidents between 1776 and 1974: a review of biographical sources. J Nerv Ment Dis. 2006 Jan;194(1):47-51. doi: 10.1097/01.nmd.0000195309.17887.f5. PMID: 16462555.

Dreadful Railroad Accident: Loss Of Life Narrow Escape Of Gen. Pierce. New York Daily Tribune. Jan 7 1853, p.5.

Dreadful Railroad Accident: Loss Of Life Narrow Escape Of Gen. Pierce. New York Daily Times, Jan 7, 1853 p. 1.

Dreadful Railroad Accident: Loss Of Life Narrow Escape Of Gen. Pierce. New York Daily Times, Jan 12, 1853 p. 1.

Dr. Bandy X. Lee. YouTube: Top Psychiatrist Sounds Alarm on DT Deteriorating Mental Health. Term: shared psychosis. The Vindication of Bandy Lee, Mother Jones magazine.

Exploring Abraham Lincoln's 'Melancholy'. By Robert Siegel, October 26, 2005 Heard on All Things Considered. Retrieved from https://www.npr.org/2005/ 10/26/4976127/exploring-abraham-lincolns-melancholy

Goode, Erica. "Arnold Hutschnecker, 102, Therapist to Nixon." The New York Times, 3 Jan. 2001.

Guide to the Nixon Family Collection (1909-1967). Richard Nixon Presidential Library and Museum.

Jack Dreyfus. A Remarkable Medicine Has Been Overlooked (1968).

Joshua Wolf Shenk, author of Lincoln's Melancholy: How Depression Challenged a President and Fueled His Greatness.

Library of Congress photographs.

NELSON, MICHAEL. "JAMES DAVID BARBER AND THE PSYCHOLOGICAL PRESIDENCY." The Virginia Quarterly Review, vol. 56, no. 4, 1980, pp. 650–67. JSTOR, http://www.jstor.org/stable/26436113 Accessed 9 Aug. 2024.

Records of the White House Office. Retrieved from https://www.archives.gov/ research/guide-fed-records/groups/130.html

Richard Nixon: The Life by John A. Farrell. Retrieved from https://www.vqronline.org/richard-nixon-revisited

The Adams Family: Triumphs and Groans. Retrieved from International Bipolar Foundation website: https://ibpf.org/the-adams-family-triumphs-and-groans/

The derailment of Franklin Pierce. By Jacob Appel, New York, New York, United States. Retrieved from https://hekint.org/2021/03/26/the-derailment-of-franklin-pierce/

The Expatriation of Franklin Pierce by Garry Boulard, November 21, 2023 Retrieved from https://maniadelight.com/2023/11/21/the-expatriation-of-franklin-pierce-by-garry-boulard/

The most narcissistic U.S. presidents. By Rich Morin, November 14, 2013. Pew Research Center. Retrieved from https://www.mcleanhospital.org/npd-provider-guide#:~:text=NPD%20in%20DSM%2D5,meet%20the%20diagnosis[1]

The Personal Memoirs of U.S. Grant, Ulysses Simpson Grant, Dover Publications (1885).

The Road to Appomattox, Robert Hendrickson, John Wiley & Sons; and the websites of the Ulysses S. Grant Home Page and Ulysses S. Grant Association. Retrieved from https://www.grantcottage.org/blog/2020/3/16/do-as-i-do

TIM WEINER. Timeline: That Time the Middle East Exploded—and Nixon Was Drunk. June 15, 2015. Retrieved from https://www.politico.com/magazine/story/2015/06/richard-nixon-watergate-drunk-yom-kippur-war-119021/

Understanding and managing somatoform disorders: Making sense of non-sense. By Roy Abraham Kallivayalil and Varghese P. Punnoose. Retrieved from https://www.ncbi.nlm.nih.gov/pmc/articles/PMC3146190/#:~:text=The%20term%20somatoform%20disorders%20was,proposed[2].

---

1. https://www.mcleanhospital.org/
   npd-provider-guide#_853ae90f0351324bd73ea615e6487517__4c761f170e016836ff84498202b99827__85
   3ae90f0351324bd73ea615e6487517_text_43ec3e5dee6e706af7766fffea512721_NPD_0bcef9c45bd8a48ed
   a1b26eb0c61c869_20in_0bcef9c45bd8a48eda1b26eb0c61c869_20DSM_0bcef9c45bd8a48eda1b26eb0c61
   c869_2D5_c0cb5f0fcf239ab3d9c1fcd31fff1efc_meet_0bcef9c45bd8a48eda1b26eb0c61c869_20the_0bcef9c
   45bd8a48eda1b26eb0c61c869_20diagnosis_0bcef9c45bd8a48eda1b26eb0c61c869_20of_0bcef9c45bd8a48
   eda1b26eb0c61c869_20NPD

2. https://www.ncbi.nlm.nih.gov/pmc/articles/
   PMC3146190/#_853ae90f0351324bd73ea615e6487517__4c761f170e016836ff84498202b99827__853ae9
   0f0351324bd73ea615e6487517_text_43ec3e5dee6e706af7766fffea512721_The_0bcef9c45bd8a48eda1b26e
   b0c61c869_20term_0bcef9c45bd8a48eda1b26eb0c61c869_20somatoform_0bcef9c45bd8a48eda1b26eb0c6
   1c869_20disorders_0bcef9c45bd8a48eda1b26eb0c61c869_20was_c0cb5f0fcf239ab3d9c1fcd31fff1efc_prop
   osed_0bcef9c45bd8a48eda1b26eb0c61c869_20categories_0bcef9c45bd8a48eda1b26eb0c61c869_20like_0b
   cef9c45bd8a48eda1b26eb0c61c869_20somatization_0bcef9c45bd8a48eda1b26eb0c61c869_20disorder

Vamik Volkan, Norman Itzkowitz, Andrew Dod. Richard Nixon: A Psychobiography (1997). Princeton University, Near Eastern Studies Department.

War of the Rebellion (military cables, official correspondence).

Watts, A. L., Lilienfeld, S. O., Smith, S. F., Miller, J. D., Campbell, W. K., Waldman, I. D., Rubenzer, S. J., & Faschingbauer, T. J. (2013). The Double-Edged Sword of Grandiose Narcissism: Implications for Successful and Unsuccessful Leadership Among U.S. Presidents. Psychological Science, 24(12), 2379-2389. https://doi.org/10.1177/0956797613491970

What We Can Learn from Abraham Lincoln's Struggle with Depression. By Rich Barlow, February 27, 2023. Boston University. Retrieved from https://www.bu.edu/articles/2023/lincoln-struggled-depression-what-we-can-learn/

Don't miss out!

Visit the website below and you can sign up to receive emails whenever Joseph Collins publishes a new book. There's no charge and no obligation.

https://books2read.com/r/B-A-ISLCB-MZISD

BOOKS 2 READ

Connecting independent readers to independent writers.

About the Author

Joseph Collins is an American writer and retired healthcare professional. What sets Joseph apart from other history and historical fiction content creators is his unique background and expertise. With former careers as a mental health counselor and Defense Intelligence Analyst, Joseph brings a depth of understanding to his storytelling that delves into the emotional and psychological motivations of historical characters, as well as their place in history. Joseph's keen insight into military conflict, intelligence services and political intrigue further enriches his storytelling. This allows him to create narratives that not only inform but also resonate on a deeply human level. His focus on historical periods such as the American Civil War, World Wars I/II and other important eras showcases his expertise in these areas, making his work both educational and engaging for history enthusiasts and casual readers alike.

Read more at https://www.nightwriterjoseph.com.